GW00578258

Be kind to you x

This book belongs to

_____

You are
good enough

Dedicated to:
My gorgeous, good enough girls: Mia and Georgia

Mean Little Cow

By Michala Leyland
With Georgia Leyland

Illustrated by Mia Leyland

First published in 2020
Copyright Wood for the Trees Coaching © 2020

ISBN: 978-1-9163844-0-8

see you on the other side of the woods......

Wood For The Trees Coaching

TEAM AUTHOR UK
Publishing with you

Mean Little Cow

By Michala Leyland
with Georgia Leyland

Illustrated by Mia Leyland

Introduction

By Michala Leyland

All of us have an inner critic voice. It's the voice you can hear telling you: 'That's not good enough.' 'You can't do that.' 'Who do you think you are trying that?' In some people it is very loud and in others it is a bit sneaky and quieter, but it still can stop you feeling good about you. It can stop you from trying new things or have you living in fear of getting things wrong. I wrote this book because for a long time my sneaky, inner critic voice was being really mean to me and I didn't realise it. That's why I named it the 'Mean Little Cow' (no offense to cows, they are sweet, peaceful animals really). That 'Mean Little Cow' voice stopped me feeling good about me and it had me feeling scared to make a mistake. Even as I grew up and became an adult.

Then one day, I decided I'd had enough of it holding me back and stopping me from enjoying my many successes, because despite that 'cow's voice' I was able to do some pretty great things with my life. However, I knew I could do so much more if I could understand how this voice worked. I decided to discover why it was doing this to me, what I could do to stop it and now I want to share that with you.

Yes, YOU! You are smart, imaginative, funny, caring, thoughtful, giddy, creative and very loveable. I want you to be able to create a long list of back chat to your inner critic. Your 'Mean Little Cow'. Or maybe you will call it something else. Something like 'Boris' or 'The Horrid Headache'. Whatever name that helps you recognise it and take away its control from holding you back from doing great things in your life.

If it tells you that you can't and shouldn't perform on stage, tell it that it is wrong and why.
If it tells you that you aren't cool enough to hang out with a particular group, tell it that it is wrong and why.
If it tells you that you are rubbish at drawing, tell it that it is wrong and why.

That's exactly what I told my eldest daughter Mia when I asked her to illustrate this book and she said she wasn't good enough. She loves drawing and particularly anime-style characters. I love how she's improving every time she puts pencil to paper. I have no idea if she's good for her age (she was 12 when she completed these pictures)

or if they are really true to the anime-style. What I do know is that at each draft she got better. When she made a mistake, she started again and didn't give up. Each time she put pen to paper I could see her body relax as she went into a flow-like state where she was in her element drawing and creating. I'm so proud of her for going out of her comfort zone and being willing to be published for all the world to see. She is exploring her talents in lots of different areas and she will find her way to what she loves and what she is good at.

I also wanted to involve my youngest daughter. She's also very creative and I'd put her head to head with any professional interior designer any day. She knows exactly how to create a mood board and moves her furniture around every few months to create a new feel to her bedroom. She's also very loving and thoughtful with her friends, so I thought she could write you a little letter to help you on days when the 'Mean Little Cow' voice is being cruel to you. She can be the self-loving voice you need to hear whilst you develop your own.

Whilst the 'Mean Little Cow' tale starts off in quite a dark way, it's a tale of hope and of growth. It's a story that will help you tap into that self-loving voice that has a different truth to the one 'Mean Little Cow' wants you to believe. It will help you remove the labels that sometimes well-meaning grownups place on you. I know because I've done it to my children from time to time and I do my best to not do it, as I know it feeds the 'Mean Little Cow's' evidence bank. I'm not perfect. Parents make mistakes too.

I hope by the end of this book you will be able to hear that self-love voice more clearly and use the technique I give you at the back of the book and Georgia's letter to you to answer it back on days it's not being nice to you.

Be kind to you.

Michala, Mia and Georgia xxx

I would like to publicly thank a Liverpool based charity for investing in the first publication of this book. Liverpool Heartbeat has been inspiring young people in the Northwest and Merseyside to pursue healthy, exciting, fulfilled lifestyles since its formation in 2002. Founded by the big-hearted Robin Baynes, MBE, the charity continues to support local youth organisations and projects for young people across the region. They have raised hundreds of thousands of pounds and invested every penny back into the community. I feel honoured to be one of the projects they have decided to support this year.

www.liverpoolheartbeat.com

The 'Mean Little Cow' popped into my head.
"You're bad, you're sad," to me, she said.

I heard that voice; it felt so true.
I heard that voice; she made me blue.

The 'Mean Little Cow' carried on.
"You think you can do that? I think you are wrong."

I heard that voice; it made me slump.
I heard that voice; it felt like a thump.

She watched me as I stood on stage.
"You're not so good, you're not so brave."

I heard that voice; I took her cue.
I heard that voice; from the stage I flew.

The 'Mean Little Cow' became louder and louder.
"You aren't so bright OR brave!" I didn't doubt her.

I heard that voice; I dropped my head.
I heard that voice; I was filled with dread.

But somewhere deep inside of me,
Another voice said, "Listen to me."

"That 'Mean Little Cow' doesn't speak true!
Here are all the things I love about you."

I heard that voice; she made me grin.
I heard that voice; over that cow's din.

"You're bright, you're funny, you are kind at your best.
You're mischievous, you're amusing, you're as good as all the rest."

I heard that voice; she made me giggle.
I heard that voice, saw 'Mean Little Cow' wriggle.

"You love, you share, you lead, you sing.
You paint, you draw, you hop, you are trying!"

I heard that voice; I looked to the sky.
I heard that voice, as I watched 'Mean Little Cow' shy.

"You're loved, you are loveable through and through.
See all of the people who do love you."

I heard that voice; it felt warm inside.
I heard that voice; I had nothing to hide.

"I know I try. I know I do.
'Mean Little Cow'... I don't need you."
"I'll get it wrong and that's ok.
I'll learn from my mistakes along the way."

"I'll try new things, it won't be good.
I'll make mistakes, just like you should."

I heard that voice; it cast its spell.
I heard that voice and all is well.

I know when I can and I know when I will.
I know what's good and when I've had my fill.

"Goodbye Little Cow, I'm simply me.
Goodbye Little Cow, that's good enough you see!"

For additional information on the inner critic and the impact on children for Parents and Educators please go to http://bit.ly/MeanLCow

About the Author

This book literally came flowing out of me one Sunday morning as I sat outside early in the morning with a cup of tea. I'd recently been on a book writing workshop, delivered by children's author Jude Lennon, and it planted a seed in my mind that I'd love to write a book that helped young people manage that part of their brain that holds so many people back. Low and behold, this 'Mean Little Cow' story came pouring out of me.

One of the tools that I use with my adult clients, as a Performance and Mindset Coach, is a technique I use with my own children, if they are struggling with that internal voice.

I'd love to share it with you in order for you to use it yourself and/or share it with your children as a tool they can use for life.

I'll give you an example of a real scenario I had with one of my girls (with her permission of course).

My eldest has been learning to play guitar and really enjoys being part of the school ensemble. It was coming up for the first school Winter performance and nerves started to get the better of her. She started to doubt herself and started listening to that 'Mean Little Cow' voice.

One evening I went into her room and she was looking very sad and agitated. 'What's wrong my love?' I asked her.

At first she wouldn't tell me, but after a big hug she started to talk.

'I'm so scared Mum. I'm the only Year 7 in the group and I'm rubbish. I can't do the performance and I'm going to look stupid. I'll make a fool of myself and the older girls will think I'm a complete idiot.'

'Is this what you have been telling yourself?' I replied. 'What did your guitar teacher say about your performance?' I asked.

'He said I was good and to keep practicing. But he's only being nice and I'm going to look completely stupid.'

Having taken a deep breath I asked my daughter, 'Is

that true? What is the actual truth here? How many weeks is it to the performance?'

'It's 3 weeks.'

'Three weeks. So, you have 3 more weeks to do as much practice as you can, is that true?'

'Yes.'

'Is it true that you have made huge progress from what you knew and how you played only two weeks ago?'

'Yes.'

'So, is it true that if you plan-in practice time and enjoy learning the pieces you have to perform, there is no reason you can't be prepared and confident to do the Winter Show? And isn't it true that you are doing this for fun because you want to learn and so you don't have to be perfect to join in?'

'It is true, I suppose.'

'Ok, so what will you do to start and what will you say to that 'Mean Little Cow' voice if it starts telling you that you are rubbish and that you can't do it?'

'I'll tell it I've got 3 weeks to practice and that I'm doing my best. I'll tell it that it's my first performance with guitar and that I'm learning, so it can be quiet and let me get on with it.'

We both smiled and I left her to it. Oh, and having taken time over the next few weeks to practice, she was fantastic at the performance! Best of all, she really enjoyed it and felt a great sense of pride in herself that she'd stuck with it DESPITE the 'Mean Little Cow' voice putting her off.

The process works as follows:

1. Listen to the Mean Little Cow voice. What is she/he/it saying?
2. Is there any truth? If so, be honest with yourself, but not nasty.
3. What is your self-loving voice saying about the situation?
4. What action will you take now?

This simple 4-step technique can really help your child to cultivate a growth mindset where making mistakes, learning and growing are all part of being a great human. Help them to cultivate this and they will thank you for years to come. Use it yourself and tame your inner critic. It's a powerful tool, I promise.

Be kind to you.

Michala Leyland, Performance and Mindset Coach

www.woodforthetreescoaching.co.uk

f @woodforthetreescoaching
@wfttcoaching
@wfttcoaching

A Letter from your Best Friend's Voice

By Georgia Leyland

Dear .... (add your name here)

I've heard you've been feeling a bit down lately and that 'Mean Little Cow voice' has been calling you names and telling you that you aren't good enough. Well, I'd like to remind you how great you are. So, here are things I love about you ...

You are kind to your friends and family. You are funny. You are gorgeous inside and out. You are caring, loving and an amazing person and you are there for others, so I am here for you, inside of you, when you need me.

If you stop believing in how great you are, when you need my help the most, listen to MY voice, and don't believe everything the 'Mean Little Cow voice' has to say. Hear my voice and you'll be happier and love yourself more.

Try to focus on all the good things about you, there are lots you know.

As you grow up, you'll make mistakes, learn from them and get better, but don't be mean to yourself and say, 'I'm rubbish' or 'I'm not good at that'. Say, 'I made a mistake and I'll learn from it', or 'I'm not good at that YET'! Learn from your mistakes and you'll become better and better. That will make you stronger, I promise.

You are loved, loveable and loving. Don't forget it.

Love from,

Your Best Friend's Voice

xxxx

Printed in Great Britain
by Amazon